About the Author

Zuzanna Bartnicka is a young author who enjoys experimenting with words. She is a poet with a vivid imagination and a metaphorical sense of writing. Her rhyming may not be obvious, but the poems she creates are invariably melodious. Zuzanna uses words to show her readers that circumstances may sometimes differ if we look at them from another perspective. Therefore, she encourages us to think deeply, feel more clearly, and use our imaginations so we could see *Beyond Life Verses*.

Beyond Life Verses

Zuzanna Bartnicka

Beyond Life Verses

Vanguard Press

VANGUARD HARDBACK

© Copyright 2025
Zuzanna Bartnicka

The right of Zuzanna Bartnicka to be identified as author of this work has been asserted by her in accordance with the Copyright, Designs and Patents Act 1988.

All Rights Reserved

No reproduction, copy or transmission of this publication may be made without written permission.
No paragraph of this publication may be reproduced, copied or transmitted save with the written permission of the publisher, or in accordance with the provisions of the Copyright Act 1956 (as amended).

Any person who commits any unauthorised act in relation to this publication may be liable to criminal prosecution and civil claims for damages.

A CIP catalogue record for this title is available from the British Library.

ISBN 978-1-83794-922-9

This is a work of fiction. Names, characters, businesses, places, events and incidents are either the products of the author's imagination or used in a fictitious manner. Any resemblance to actual persons, living or dead, or actual events is purely coincidental.

*Vanguard Press is an imprint of
Pegasus Elliot Mackenzie Publishers Ltd.*
www.pegasuspublishers.com

First Published in 2025

**Vanguard Press
Sheraton House Castle Park
Cambridge England**

Printed & Bound in Great Britain

Dedication

To my dearest family and friends for always supporting me, and to my grandparents, without whom my dream wouldn't have come true.

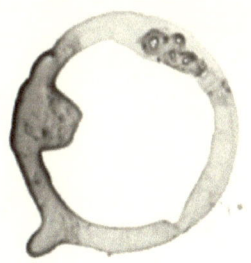

Dear Reader,

I wrote this book of consolidated thoughts to give you a glimpse into life from my perspective. I wanted to share with you some lessons life gave me and rhyme conclusions I reached from them. But before you dive into the abyss of poetry, here's one last thing I want to say:

For as long as I can remember, I've tried to hide who I really am by mirroring those around me. Fearing I would be too much, I shielded myself behind thick paper walls, afraid of being judged. Yet, life has taught me a profound truth: beneath their facades, everyone dreads revealing their true sides.

So, I encourage you—Dear Reader—to be true to who you are and stand up for what you believe in. For it is easier to hide, but it demands courage to exhibit your true colors in a world filled with shades of gray.

I hope you will find joy in the journey I created for you among these pages.

"Embrace the journey and its flaws."
Zuzanna Bartnicka

Waltz

Innocent glance,
eyes meet in a dance,
putting us in state
of eternal grace.
Beneath the sunrise,
whispers unfold,
deepest desires,
stories to be told.

Time Trap

Childhood went away
in a blink of an eye.
How am I supposed
to be adult now?
Stay warm
in this cold world,
where its seriousness
fills my veins,
making me pretend
to blend in just great.

Too much responsibility,
I can't take it all.
it's blurring my vision
of joy I held upon.

There are days that I wish
there was a reverse card,
so I could one last time
believe in Santa's guard.

Shifting Desires

When we grow up,
we only see beginnings.

Oh, Mom!
I want to be a dancer,
forgetting about it the next day.

Oh, Dad!
I want to be a president,
unable to make good sentence.

Oh, Gram!
I want to be a painter,
not thinking about the rent pay.

But what we thought about
was our happiness
and peaceful heart.

So let your dreams evolve,
'cause life was much brighter
when you had idea for it all.

Deadly Timer

Time is the only
ally of death,
powerful enough
to take away
our sorrows.

Four Seasons of Life

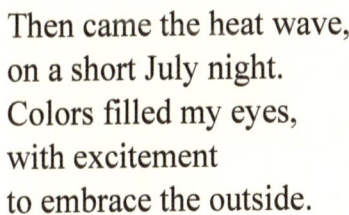

Rising like a snowdrop,
birds develop their glop.
When first sun ray
cuts window slot,
changing time's course.

Then came the heat wave,
on a short July night.
Colors filled my eyes,
with excitement
to embrace the outside.

I didn't get to blink
before orange appeared
out of nowhere.
I felt the chill—
Spooky Time is here.

Water's getting hard.
People start to glide.
Hot chocolate,
thick blanket,
on December's long night.

And that's the circle of life—
so find beauty in each part,
'cause it's too short
to look for flaws
where growth could be pulled on.

Until We Meet Again

I want to stop smiling
when I see your face,
but there's something
deep inside
telling me
I should be there.

Everything feels at peace
when I see your eyes.
World is quiet,
mind is clear,
heart rate drops
when I feel your touch.

You could never
bore me with
the stories and fun facts,
'cause despite
your body,
I love your mind.

Talking with you
puts a hold
on a clock
and makes me forget
why I was sad before.

Your hug
reminds me of home,
so I can bury
my feelings,
if that means
I could hold you
for a second more.

No "Right" Time

Take the leap,
try yourself,
encourage to change
what was meant to stay
the same.

Growth show in time,
but don't stand by,
waiting for
the "right" to come.

Your hopes and dreams
aren't there to stay,
so you must strive
to make them happen.

In due time,
inevitable fall will come.
Past will rush
through your mind.

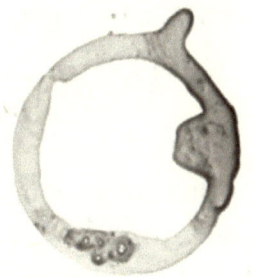

Don't be scared
of that day,
but remember
to live a little,
so it could be the best.

One Last Time

I never thought
one day I would see
my grandma
not able to speak.

I never thought
that conversation
could be the last
we've ever got.

I thought
I could visit you
on Sunday lunch,
sit and hear the stories
one more time.

I thought
that hug was
a "see you later" one,
not a goodbye.

But here I am,
sitting in a dark room
at three a.m.,
wishing I could hear
your laugh again.

All I have now
is a memory
that I cherish inside,
not ready to let go
of what once felt
so interminable.

You Matter

Someone sees a sunset,
wanting to share it with you.
Someone smells a flower,
hoping to give it to you.

Someone goes to party,
wishing to dance with you.
Someone lays in bed at night,
longing to talk to you.

Someone reads a book,
reminding them of you.
Someone took a walk,
remembering how they strolled with you.

Never underestimate
how important you are.

Have a Great Day

Smile—
life is precious
Be proud—
you've overcome so much.

Stay positive—
glass is half-filled.
Don't stress
over little things.

Look around,
kill them with a smile.
That's your superpower—
never out of style.

Flux

Blind need to
feel seen—accepted by
shifting reality.

Embers of Understanding

Love is a friendship on fire,
understanding shared
in the darkest of hours.

Sneaking out to see
how the sun rises,
telling each other's
deepest desires.

Because love is more than a feeling—
it's a state of constant being,
that helpless smirk
right after the eyes meet.

Long hugs
before falling asleep,
Pinky promises
never to be broken.

Show affection
of true devotion.
It's dancing in the kitchen,
spilling tea
over cup of coffee.

Playing chess,
as if life depend
on a game of hearts
that will never end.

But most importantly, love
is when life begins to rumble
and they're your light in the tunnel.

Life is a Chessboard

We make sacrifices to win
the game of passion and strategy.
We count our steps
on the way to end,
forgetting opponent
wants to win as well.

Moving wisely
toward the king,
guarded by rocks,
rising higher
to protect our dreams.

Feeling confident,
we move ahead,
but here comes a knight,
full of turns and twists,
ruining position,
punching with its fists.

Then out of nowhere,
bishop appears,
striking momentarily,
reflecting connections
inside human mind.

Like pawns, we advance
strategically taking
step by step toward end,
and when we think
all is foregone,
the queen rises steadily,
changing entire course.

Checkmates and gambits,
triumphs and falls,
life's chessboard
hold stories among its walls.

In this complex game,
where moves are defined,
life's journey unfolds,
creating prospects,
showing tapestry of the human mind.

Take Me Back

Cozy sweater,
one you loved most,
brings back memories
of hot chocolate and ghosts.

Midnight stories,
when stargazing for more,
freedom you gave me
to explore the unexplored.

You taught me compassion
for those of need
and never doubted
I would succeed.

And now I see your spark
drifting away quicker than sound.

Forget-Me-Not Flower

Your effortless blue
reminds me of the way you lie.
When you bloom before my eyes,
you can't see further than your stalk.

Allegiance you held upon me
blinded me enough
to believe you could be the one.

True Love

For a little while,
I was yours and you were mine.
You filled my void of sadness
with smiles I didn't know would matter.

And I drowned in your imperfections,
which made me love you even harder.

Art of Perspective

Love isn't blind;
it shows perspective over time.

The rocky road full of mistakes
teaches us about ourselves.
We want to grow together,
so we work to be better.

The successful relationship is the one
we create with tears, long nights, and smiles.
But after many ups and downs,
we lay in bed and laugh.

And we feel like we belong
in a place we so call home.

Imperfect Affection

The love I write about
is pure but hard to find.

If you look for perfection,
love is not your direction.

It starts with butterflies
but ends up being rough.
We need to sacrifice
the certain parts of life
so as to build connection
that survives any aversion.

Lovely Hatred

I hate when you are
hot and cold,
with no reason.
One day you're here,
the next you disappear.

I hate that I smile
the moment I see you,
and when you leave,
all I want is you near.

It's been a while now,
since our eyes met,
but each morning
I wake up thinking,
Maybe there's still a chance.

But then I saw you
with her by your side.
Fuck…
I hate it when I see
you're happier without me.

Gone With the Wind

Smell of cloves,
sunshine on my lips,
old book on the shelf,
pictures in my head.

It crushes my heart,
'cause they'll never feel the same.

Airport Muddle

I wander through alleys
of possibilities and cold showers.
I look around to find myself
standing at the edge of panic.

My heart ripped in half,
one ahead, one behind.
But where am I now?

Grief

Void in my heart,
never to be filled,
reminds me of someone
I used to grow up with.

Time
is what took you
from my side
to the ground.

Looking back,
I never thought
six feet would feel
so far.

And yet I stood there
15th of May,
touching your
cold hand,
wishing for your lungs
to fill
once again.

And even though
I know
you lived your life
to the fullest,
I can't help but think
how unlucky
my kids will be
to never know your spirit.

My Silent Hero

I grew up
in a house
with no dad.

My dad
wasn't there…
he shield behind
computer screens,
avoiding conversations
with me.

My whole life
I held the anger
up my throat…
mad to know
I grew up
in a house
with no dad.

But my dad
was always there…
he worked late,
with sleeping pills
next his bed,
for me.

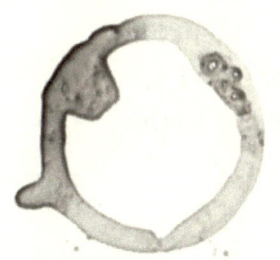

My dad
is a man
of action…
with no words
to share,
yet he's always there.

My whole life
I believed
he hated me…
his absent scent
was louder
than his presence.

But my dad
loves me…
wishing me the best.
He barely slept,
working late,
for me.

My dad
is a silent hero…
for now I see
he did all that
for me.

Adulthood

We do things we hate
to fulfill someone's dream.
We complain about fate,
forgetting we hold the strings.

Driven by ambitions,
we escape reality,
wishing better tomorrow
will appear in instant glimpse.

Never Enough

We seek grand gestures,
big declarations,
constantly insufficient
for appreciation.

In this never-ending story
of needing, not giving,
we start to turn into
people with no feelings.

Modern World

We overstimulate ourselves
with a box in our hands,
forgetting that dopamine
isn't always our friend.

Each morning we decide
to close our eyes and hide
in a digital world
we feel so welcomed for.

That's why we're addicted
to the thing that divides us
from reality and fiction.

Gratiam

Vulnerable,
I was
when you found me
that night.

You stepped into
my wounded heart,
unaware
of what's inside.

I opened up,
you let me in,
and that's how
our story begun.

First chapter,
we unlocked with fire,
passion filled
the room,
leaving no place
for sadness.

Morning breath,
fast lunch breaks,
music playing
in the dark,
where we spent
most time.

Next chapter
was when
our bodies
took a break,
giving space
for our minds
to connect and dance.

Pity
is what you felt
for me back then.
Wanting to be the hero,
you tried
putting back the pieces
of my heart.

I,
on the other hand,
saw your soul—
cotton pure,
poisoned by people
who made you
so cold.

In due time,
the pity was gone,
realizing
our hearts
had connection
of some kind.

next chapter
was tough…
there were
no more butterflies.
Life punched us
with long distance,
less contact,
more cries.

And it was harder
for our hearts
to stay as they are,
but here came
the moment
so longed for us both.

We fell into
each other's arms,
and for split second,
our hearts
were whole once more.

Last chapter
is where
our story comes to end.
After almost
two years,
we vanished
as if the pity we felt
was once again there.

But this time,
the pity meant something else.
We changed
we matured,
realizing we can't
hold our hearts
in a never-ending game.

The stake was too high,
the emotions too dry,
so we let go of the love
we so badly searched for.

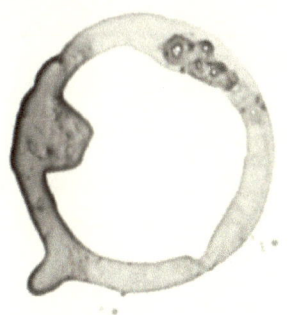

Wishing the Past

I wish we've never met,
so I wouldn't miss your smile.
I look at old pictures,
wanting to go back in time.
I wish I never knew
all these sides of you,
'cause time makes me miss
all pieces of you.

I wish I never said
all these hurtful words.
Though they were true,
it doesn't change fact
that I love you.

Not Enough

Close enough,
and yet not
together.

Watching night sky,
holding hands,
in my dreams we're
~ infinite ~

In my dreams, we're
holding hands,
watching night sky
together,
and yet not
close enough.

Lost in the Memories

When I look in the mirror,
I see a young lost kid.
I'm almost twenty,
but feeling like I'm stuck at twelve.

Sick of waiting,
figuring shit out,
I want to go back
to the good old times.

I miss the old days
when our worry was where to go have fun.
I miss the old days
when we lived each day like it was our last one.
I miss the old days
when we had joy, and we were innocent.
I'd give it all to live that life again.

We said forever—
how naïve we were.
All these plans,
the laughs I can't forget.

Being here alone feels wrong,
but I know we are long gone,
so I let memories fly this one last time
before a final goodbye.

I miss the old days
when dreams weren't out of reach for us.
I miss the old days
when a glass of wine meant fun.
I miss the old days
when everything felt peaceful and simple.
I'd give it all to feel that way again.

In Differences United

"We are no different," they said,
looking for a reason to divide instead.

The biggest lie I was told
is that every life matters—ditto.
Black, Mexican, yellow, white,
they made us think only one is right.

But is it true? Is it though?
Or is it just easier to hate than let go…

Forget about past, have a fresh start,
open our eyes to reality around.
Rewrite what was written with hate, disrespect,
unite as four equals, and our rights—protect.

Painterly Expressed

To paint
is to find a
way to express that which
is unexpressed—hidden
deeply inside.

Anguished Mind

In constant search
for souls to touch,
feel pressure
of warmth,
filling bodies
from inside out.

For a bit
of affection,
we do things we despise,
not realizing back then
they could ruin
our lives.

"Just five minutes,"
he said,
revealing what's
hidden in his pants.

I did feel pressure,
but in fairytales
they said "yes" first.

Five minutes
never felt so long.
My screams
never so silent.

And for first time,
no one would come,
get me out
and make it stop.

Taking my body,
as if it wasn't mine,
made me feel
like impostor
in my own mind.

For five minutes,
he managed to
hold time,
aware his pleasure
will make me
lose spirit for life.

I cried
like I never did before,
begging him to stop,
but his ears
were dull.

In these five minutes,
my whole life
collapsed.
My self-image
never recovered
after my body
stopped being mine.

Every seven years,
all the cells change,
so I have only few more
to live in a body
he hasn't touched before.

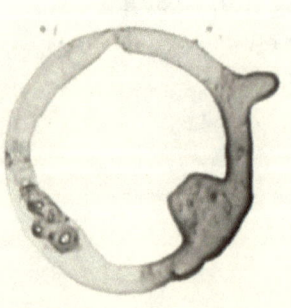

Let It Go

Past is long foregone
to undone things
is not an option.

Grab your lessons,
hold them close
never wish memories
to be gone.

If not for the past,
mirror wouldn't recognize
face you have now.

So smile, my dear,
let it go,
grateful for
the path you follow.

Ode to Free Will

I question my right—
acting, thinking—
whether you even exist.

Centuries of wonder, undermining
your endlessness ability to persist.

In ongoing reality
of manipulating, persuading,
where humans no longer insist
on being free, I am asking—
Do you even exist?

No More…

When I grow up,
I want to be good,
find myself and heal my wounds.
I want to make a difference,
spread love and tell my truth.

My dreams,
crushed under their reality,
where you can be bought,
where your life isn't precious.

From the moment you're born,
your free will is gone.
Freedom of speech?
Stay quiet, or they make you so.

Don't be too good.
Don't be too perfect,
or they'll see you as a threat.
Right to liberty, property, and life?
Maybe on paper, but never applied.

They give us illusions of being free,
but in the end, they pull the strings.

When I was young,
I believed people are good,
filled with intentions that are pure.
I believed I could make a difference,
break the circle of misuse.

Earth is our home,
most generous of all hosts,
sadly, people have a habit
of overusing hospitality
of our planet.

There will be a day when cold shower
strike us with the lack of power.
We will open our eyes in fury
and realize that we can't eat money.

Do we need to know this pain
to understand our actions will deprive
our life, liberty, and property rights?

And the worst part of it
is that my words won't change a thing.

I Am Just Doing Me

My inner voice,
calling that it's time to go,
start a new chapter
away from home.

Self-doubt…
Afraid life won't let me pass,
write my own story, and make it count.

Fearless…
And yet full of doubt,
whether my plans are worth to hazard.

Hopeful…
Even though the ending's not clear,
I'll take that first step,
see where it gets me.

I'm Just a Human

We make decisions
based on emotions.
We let our guard down,
making bad choices.

We give our hearts
into wrong hands.
We say too much
when we should say less.

We build and break things.
We jump and go down.
We are human beings,
just living our lives.

Sharp Edge

That sound
when sharp meets blunt,
leaving snowflakes behind,
peacefully spinning on the edge
of dreams.

Opposite Synergy

Women are from Venus
Men from Mars
Earth being the place
we meet and align.
At times to comprehend
the differences we share
is like breathing the Moon—
impossible and obscure.

To achieve synergy
between two
embroiled species,
compromise we seek
to catch on
what is missing.

In the end
denouement—
to cease misconception
is to fill the gap
with communication.

Temporization

"Life is short"—
it's said a lot,
yet the wording
of this sentence
is barely acknowledged.
We love excuses,
buts and because,
yet time is running
faster than we know.
Nothing starts
if nothing changes,
so go out there,
don't threat
a challenge.

Reliance

Trust your gut,
follow your heart.
They work best
when combined.
Focus on the goal,
but feel excitement
following the road.

Dragonfly

Unpleasant to some,
intriguing to others
floating above water,
it dreads for another.
My mom used to say,
don't judge
by things' cover.
Instead, come nearby,
observe and discover.
You may be ecstatic
how much you align
with someone you thought
you were nothing alike.

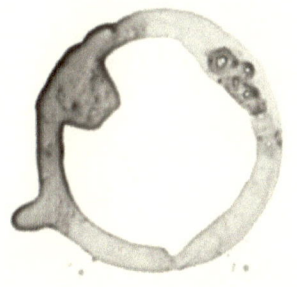

Forte

"My life ended
that day,"
that's what I said,
unaware of the doors
I crossed straight ahead.
Out of the blue,
misery
turned into
opportunity,
and I got reborn
stronger than
I've ever been
before.

Imbalance

We fall in love
and lose our minds.
We fall apart
and stick to lies.
For so-called love,
we would have died—
immune to toxins,
we lose our sight.

And as day comes,
one stormy night,
when sight is back
yet heart is rived,
begging for help,
now they've lost sight.
For so-called love,
they wouldn't die.

Non Romantic Love

Because sometimes all you need
is a friend and a cup of coffee.

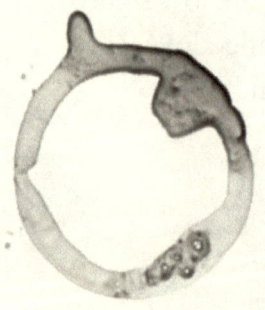

Art of Embracement

People rush through life,
blind to the little things around,
putting on masks
to hide their true sides,
wishing no one would recognize
the fear hidden inside.

We are afraid to lose time,
but we end up missing life.
So open your heart to the world,
embrace the journey and its flaws,
because the point in existence
is to dive in, not drifting.

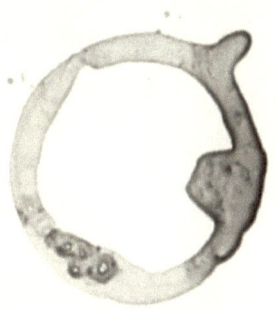

www.ingramcontent.com/pod-product-compliance
Lightning Source LLC
Chambersburg PA
CBHW030108240426
43661CB00031B/1333/J